THIS BOOK BELONGS TO

_____

MY ANNUAL SAVINGS TARGET IS:

$

MONTH

_____

_____

_____

_____

_____

_____

_____

_____

_____

_____

_____

_____

SAVINGS TARGET FOR THE MONTH

$ _____

$ _____

$ _____

$ _____

$ _____

$ _____

$ _____

$ _____

$ _____

$ _____

$ _____

$ _____

MONTH

MONTHLY INCOME

Date	Description	Amount
		$
		$
		$
		$
		$
	Total:	$

MONTHLY FIXED EXPENSES

Date	Description	Amount
		$
		$
		$
		$
		$
		$
		$
		$
		$
		$
		$
		$
		$
		$
	Total:	$

MY SAVINGS TARGET FOR THIS MONTH IS

$

MONEY AVAILABLE

Income		Fixed Expenses		Savings Goal		Money Available
	−		−		=	

ESTIMATED SPENDING MONEY

	Week 1	Week 2	Week 3	Week 4	Week 5
Date					
Estimated Spending Money					
Expenses					

NOTES

_____

_____

_____

_____

_____

EXPENSE TRACKER: WEEK 1

Date	Description	Is It Needed? (Y/N)	Amount
			$
			$
			$
			$
			$
			$
			$
			$
			$
			$
			$
			$
			$
			$
			$
			$
			$
			$
			$
			$
			$
			$
			$
			$
			$
			$
			$
		Total:	$

EXPENSE TRACKER: WEEK 2

Date	Description	Is It Needed? (Y/N)	Amount
			$
			$
			$
			$
			$
			$
			$
			$
			$
			$
			$
			$
			$
			$
			$
			$
			$
			$
			$
			$
			$
			$
			$
			$
			$
			$
		Total:	$

EXPENSE TRACKER: WEEK 3

Date	Description	Is It Needed? (Y/N)	Amount
			$
			$
			$
			$
			$
			$
			$
			$
			$
			$
			$
			$
			$
			$
			$
			$
			$
			$
			$
			$
			$
			$
			$
			$
			$
			$
			$
		Total:	$

EXPENSE TRACKER: WEEK 4

Date	Description	Is It Needed? (Y/N)	Amount
			$
			$
			$
			$
			$
			$
			$
			$
			$
			$
			$
			$
			$
			$
			$
			$
			$
			$
			$
			$
			$
			$
			$
			$
			$
			$
			$
		Total:	$

EXPENSE TRACKER: WEEK 5

Date	Description	Is It Needed? (Y/N)	Amount
			$
			$
			$
			$
			$
			$
			$
			$
			$
			$
			$
			$
			$
			$
			$
			$
			$
			$
			$
			$
			$
			$
			$
			$
			$
		Total:	$

MONTHLY REVIEW

	1. Needed	2. Not Needed	Total Spending (1+2)
Week 1			
Week 2			
Week 3			
Week 4			
Week 5			
Total			

Money Available This Month − **Total Spending This Month** = **Money Saved This Month!**

HOW WELL DID YOU DO THIS MONTH? ☆ ☆ ☆ ☆ ☆

HOW TO SAVE EVEN MORE NEXT MONTH?

_____

_____

_____

_____

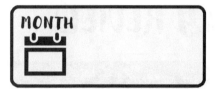

MONTH

SAVINGS ACCOUNT
(Beginning of Month)

$

MONTHLY INCOME

Date	Description	Amount
		$
		$
		$
		$
		$
	Total:	$

MONTHLY FIXED EXPENSES

Date	Description	Amount
		$
		$
		$
		$
		$
		$
		$
		$
		$
		$
		$
		$
		$
		$
		$
	Total:	$

MY SAVINGS TARGET FOR THIS MONTH IS

$

MONEY AVAILABLE

Income — Fixed Expenses — Savings Goal = Money Available

ESTIMATED SPENDING MONEY

	Week 1	Week 2	Week 3	Week 4	Week 5
Date					
Estimated Spending Money					
Expenses					

NOTES

_____

_____

_____

_____

_____

EXPENSE TRACKER: WEEK 1

Date	Description	Is It Needed? (Y/N)	Amount
			$
			$
			$
			$
			$
			$
			$
			$
			$
			$
			$
			$
			$
			$
			$
			$
			$
			$
			$
			$
			$
			$
			$
			$
			$
		Total:	$

EXPENSE TRACKER: WEEK 2

Date	Description	Is It Needed? (Y/N)	Amount
			$
			$
			$
			$
			$
			$
			$
			$
			$
			$
			$
			$
			$
			$
			$
			$
			$
			$
			$
			$
			$
			$
			$
			$
			$
			$
			$
		Total:	$

EXPENSE TRACKER: WEEK 3

Date	Description	Is It Needed? (Y/N)	Amount
			$
			$
			$
			$
			$
			$
			$
			$
			$
			$
			$
			$
			$
			$
			$
			$
			$
			$
			$
			$
			$
			$
			$
			$
			$
		Total:	$

EXPENSE TRACKER: WEEK 4

Date	Description	Is It Needed? (Y/N)	Amount
			$
			$
			$
			$
			$
			$
			$
			$
			$
			$
			$
			$
			$
			$
			$
			$
			$
			$
			$
			$
			$
			$
			$
			$
			$
			$
			$
		Total:	$

EXPENSE TRACKER: WEEK 5

Date	Description	Is It Needed? (Y/N)	Amount
			$
			$
			$
			$
			$
			$
			$
			$
			$
			$
			$
			$
			$
			$
			$
			$
			$
			$
			$
			$
			$
			$
			$
			$
			$
			$
		Total:	$

MONTHLY REVIEW

	1. Needed	2. Not Needed	Total Spending (1+2)
Week 1			
Week 2			
Week 3			
Week 4			
Week 5			
Total			

Money Available This Month − **Total Spending This Month** = **Money Saved This Month!**

HOW WELL DID YOU DO THIS MONTH? ☆☆☆☆☆

HOW TO SAVE EVEN MORE NEXT MONTH?

_____

_____

_____

_____

MONTH

MONTHLY INCOME

Date	Description	Amount
		$
		$
		$
		$
		$
	Total:	$

MONTHLY FIXED EXPENSES

Date	Description	Amount
		$
		$
		$
		$
		$
		$
		$
		$
		$
		$
		$
		$
		$
	Total:	$

MY SAVINGS TARGET FOR THIS MONTH IS

$

MONEY AVAILABLE

Income		Fixed Expenses		Savings Goal		Money Available
☐	−	☐	−	☐	=	☐

ESTIMATED SPENDING MONEY

	Week 1	Week 2	Week 3	Week 4	Week 5
Date					
Estimated Spending Money					
Expenses					

NOTES

_____

_____

_____

_____

_____

EXPENSE TRACKER: WEEK 1

Date	Description	Is It Needed? (Y/N)	Amount
			$
			$
			$
			$
			$
			$
			$
			$
			$
			$
			$
			$
			$
			$
			$
			$
			$
			$
			$
			$
			$
			$
			$
			$
			$
		Total:	$

EXPENSE TRACKER: WEEK 2

Date	Description	Is It Needed? (Y/N)	Amount
			$
			$
			$
			$
			$
			$
			$
			$
			$
			$
			$
			$
			$
			$
			$
			$
			$
			$
			$
			$
			$
			$
			$
			$
			$
			$
			$
		Total:	$

EXPENSE TRACKER: WEEK 3

Date	Description	Is It Needed? (Y/N)	Amount
			$
			$
			$
			$
			$
			$
			$
			$
			$
			$
			$
			$
			$
			$
			$
			$
			$
			$
			$
			$
			$
			$
			$
			$
			$
			$
			$
			$
		Total:	$

EXPENSE TRACKER: WEEK 4

Date	Description	Is It Needed? (Y/N)	Amount
			$
			$
			$
			$
			$
			$
			$
			$
			$
			$
			$
			$
			$
			$
			$
			$
			$
			$
			$
			$
			$
			$
			$
			$
			$
			$
		Total:	$

EXPENSE TRACKER: WEEK 5

Date	Description	Is It Needed? (Y/N)	Amount
			$
			$
			$
			$
			$
			$
			$
			$
			$
			$
			$
			$
			$
			$
			$
			$
			$
			$
			$
			$
			$
			$
			$
			$
			$
			$
			$
		Total:	$

MONTHLY REVIEW

	1. Needed	2. Not Needed	Total Spending (1+2)
Week 1			
Week 2			
Week 3			
Week 4			
Week 5			
Total			

Money Available This Month − **Total Spending This Month** = **Money Saved This Month!**

HOW WELL DID YOU DO THIS MONTH? ☆ ☆ ☆ ☆ ☆

HOW TO SAVE EVEN MORE NEXT MONTH?

_____

_____

_____

_____

MONTH

MONTHLY INCOME

Date	Description	Amount
		$
		$
		$
		$
		$
	Total:	$

MONTHLY FIXED EXPENSES

Date	Description	Amount
		$
		$
		$
		$
		$
		$
		$
		$
		$
		$
		$
		$
		$
		$
		$
	Total:	$

MY SAVINGS TARGET FOR THIS MONTH IS

$

MONEY AVAILABLE

Income		Fixed Expenses		Savings Goal		Money Available
☐	−	☐	−	☐	=	☐

ESTIMATED SPENDING MONEY

	Week 1	Week 2	Week 3	Week 4	Week 5
Date					
Estimated Spending Money					
Expenses					

NOTES

_____

_____

_____

_____

_____

EXPENSE TRACKER: WEEK 1

Date	Description	Is It Needed? (Y/N)	Amount
			$
			$
			$
			$
			$
			$
			$
			$
			$
			$
			$
			$
			$
			$
			$
			$
			$
			$
			$
			$
			$
			$
			$
			$
			$
			$
		Total:	$

EXPENSE TRACKER: WEEK 2

Date	Description	Is It Needed? (Y/N)	Amount
			$
			$
			$
			$
			$
			$
			$
			$
			$
			$
			$
			$
			$
			$
			$
			$
			$
			$
			$
			$
			$
			$
			$
			$
			$
			$
			$
	Total:		$

EXPENSE TRACKER: WEEK 3

Date	Description	Is It Needed? (Y/N)	Amount
			$
			$
			$
			$
			$
			$
			$
			$
			$
			$
			$
			$
			$
			$
			$
			$
			$
			$
			$
			$
			$
			$
			$
			$
			$
			$
		Total:	$

EXPENSE TRACKER: WEEK 4

Date	Description	Is It Needed? (Y/N)	Amount
			$
			$
			$
			$
			$
			$
			$
			$
			$
			$
			$
			$
			$
			$
			$
			$
			$
			$
			$
			$
			$
			$
			$
			$
			$
			$
			$
		Total:	$

EXPENSE TRACKER: WEEK 5

Date	Description	Is It Needed? (Y/N)	Amount
			$
			$
			$
			$
			$
			$
			$
			$
			$
			$
			$
			$
			$
			$
			$
			$
			$
			$
			$
			$
			$
			$
			$
			$
			$
			$
			$
		Total:	$

MONTHLY REVIEW

	1. Needed	2. Not Needed	Total Spending (1+2)
Week 1			
Week 2			
Week 3			
Week 4			
Week 5			
Total			

Money Available This Month

Total Spending This Month

Money Saved This Month!

[ ] − [ ] = [ ]

HOW WELL DID YOU DO THIS MONTH? ☆☆☆☆☆

HOW TO SAVE EVEN MORE NEXT MONTH?

_____

_____

_____

_____

MONTH

SAVINGS ACCOUNT
(Beginning of Month)

$

MONTHLY INCOME

Date	Description	Amount
		$
		$
		$
		$
		$
	Total:	$

MONTHLY FIXED EXPENSES

Date	Description	Amount
		$
		$
		$
		$
		$
		$
		$
		$
		$
		$
		$
		$
		$
		$
	Total:	$

MY SAVINGS TARGET FOR THIS MONTH IS

$

MONEY AVAILABLE

Income		Fixed Expenses		Savings Goal		Money Available
	−		−		=	

ESTIMATED SPENDING MONEY

	Week 1	Week 2	Week 3	Week 4	Week 5
Date					
Estimated Spending Money					
Expenses					

NOTES

_____

_____

_____

_____

_____

EXPENSE TRACKER: WEEK 1

Date	Description	Is It Needed? (Y/N)	Amount
			$
			$
			$
			$
			$
			$
			$
			$
			$
			$
			$
			$
			$
			$
			$
			$
			$
			$
			$
			$
			$
			$
			$
			$
			$
			$
			$
		Total:	$

EXPENSE TRACKER: WEEK 2

Date	Description	Is It Needed? (Y/N)	Amount
			$
			$
			$
			$
			$
			$
			$
			$
			$
			$
			$
			$
			$
			$
			$
			$
			$
			$
			$
			$
			$
			$
			$
			$
			$
		Total:	$

EXPENSE TRACKER: WEEK 3

Date	Description	Is It Needed? (Y/N)	Amount
			$
			$
			$
			$
			$
			$
			$
			$
			$
			$
			$
			$
			$
			$
			$
			$
			$
			$
			$
			$
			$
			$
			$
			$
			$
			$
		Total:	$

EXPENSE TRACKER: WEEK 4

Date	Description	Is It Needed? (Y/N)	Amount
			$
			$
			$
			$
			$
			$
			$
			$
			$
			$
			$
			$
			$
			$
			$
			$
			$
			$
			$
			$
			$
			$
			$
			$
			$
			$
			$
		Total:	$

EXPENSE TRACKER: WEEK 5

Date	Description	Is It Needed? (Y/N)	Amount
			$
			$
			$
			$
			$
			$
			$
			$
			$
			$
			$
			$
			$
			$
			$
			$
			$
			$
			$
			$
			$
			$
			$
			$
			$
			$
		Total:	$

MONTHLY REVIEW

	1. Needed	2. Not Needed	Total Spending (1+2)
Week 1			
Week 2			
Week 3			
Week 4			
Week 5			
Total			

Money Available This Month

Total Spending This Month

Money Saved This Month!

[ ] − [ ] = [ ]

HOW WELL DID YOU DO THIS MONTH?   ☆ ☆ ☆ ☆ ☆

HOW TO SAVE EVEN MORE NEXT MONTH?

_____

_____

_____

_____

MONTH

SAVINGS ACCOUNT
(Beginning of Month)

$

MONTHLY INCOME

Date	Description	Amount
		$
		$
		$
		$
		$
	Total:	$

MONTHLY FIXED EXPENSES

Date	Description	Amount
		$
		$
		$
		$
		$
		$
		$
		$
		$
		$
		$
		$
		$
		$
	Total:	$

MY SAVINGS TARGET FOR THIS MONTH IS

$

MONEY AVAILABLE

Income	Fixed Expenses	Savings Goal	Money Available
-	-	=	

ESTIMATED SPENDING MONEY

	Week 1	Week 2	Week 3	Week 4	Week 5
Date					
Estimated Spending Money					
Expenses					

NOTES

_____
_____
_____
_____
_____

EXPENSE TRACKER: WEEK 1

Date	Description	Is It Needed? (Y/N)	Amount
			$
			$
			$
			$
			$
			$
			$
			$
			$
			$
			$
			$
			$
			$
			$
			$
			$
			$
			$
			$
			$
			$
			$
			$
			$
			$
			$
		Total:	$

EXPENSE TRACKER: WEEK 2

Date	Description	Is It Needed? (Y/N)	Amount
			$
			$
			$
			$
			$
			$
			$
			$
			$
			$
			$
			$
			$
			$
			$
			$
			$
			$
			$
			$
			$
			$
			$
			$
			$
			$
			$
			$
		Total:	$

EXPENSE TRACKER: WEEK 3

Date	Description	Is It Needed? (Y/N)	Amount
			$
			$
			$
			$
			$
			$
			$
			$
			$
			$
			$
			$
			$
			$
			$
			$
			$
			$
			$
			$
			$
			$
			$
			$
			$
			$
			$
		Total:	$

EXPENSE TRACKER: WEEK 4

Date	Description	Is It Needed? (Y/N)	Amount
			$
			$
			$
			$
			$
			$
			$
			$
			$
			$
			$
			$
			$
			$
			$
			$
			$
			$
			$
			$
			$
			$
			$
			$
			$
			$
		Total:	$

EXPENSE TRACKER: WEEK 5

Date	Description	Is It Needed? (Y/N)	Amount
			$
			$
			$
			$
			$
			$
			$
			$
			$
			$
			$
			$
			$
			$
			$
			$
			$
			$
			$
			$
			$
			$
			$
			$
			$
			$
			$
		Total:	$

MONTHLY REVIEW

	1. Needed	2. Not Needed	Total Spending (1+2)
Week 1			
Week 2			
Week 3			
Week 4			
Week 5			
Total			

Money Available This Month

[ ] **-** [ ] **=**

Total Spending This Month

Money Saved This Month!

HOW WELL DID YOU DO THIS MONTH? ☆ ☆ ☆ ☆ ☆

HOW TO SAVE EVEN MORE NEXT MONTH?

_____

_____

_____

_____

MONTH

SAVINGS ACCOUNT
(Beginning of Month)

$

MONTHLY INCOME

Date	Description	Amount
		$
		$
		$
		$
		$
	Total:	$

MONTHLY FIXED EXPENSES

Date	Description	Amount
		$
		$
		$
		$
		$
		$
		$
		$
		$
		$
		$
		$
		$
		$
	Total:	$

MY SAVINGS TARGET FOR THIS MONTH IS

$

MONEY AVAILABLE

Income		Fixed Expenses		Savings Goal		Money Available
	−		−		=	

ESTIMATED SPENDING MONEY

	Week 1	Week 2	Week 3	Week 4	Week 5
Date					
Estimated Spending Money					
Expenses					

NOTES

_____

_____

_____

_____

_____

EXPENSE TRACKER: WEEK 1

Date	Description	Is It Needed? (Y/N)	Amount
			$
			$
			$
			$
			$
			$
			$
			$
			$
			$
			$
			$
			$
			$
			$
			$
			$
			$
			$
			$
			$
			$
			$
			$
			$
			$
			$
		Total:	$

EXPENSE TRACKER: WEEK 2

Date	Description	Is It Needed? (Y/N)	Amount
			$
			$
			$
			$
			$
			$
			$
			$
			$
			$
			$
			$
			$
			$
			$
			$
			$
			$
			$
			$
			$
			$
			$
			$
			$
		Total:	$

EXPENSE TRACKER: WEEK 3

Date	Description	Is It Needed? (Y/N)	Amount
			$
			$
			$
			$
			$
			$
			$
			$
			$
			$
			$
			$
			$
			$
			$
			$
			$
			$
			$
			$
			$
			$
			$
			$
			$
			$
		Total:	$

EXPENSE TRACKER: WEEK 4

Date	Description	Is It Needed? (Y/N)	Amount
			$
			$
			$
			$
			$
			$
			$
			$
			$
			$
			$
			$
			$
			$
			$
			$
			$
			$
			$
			$
			$
			$
			$
			$
			$
			$
			$
			$
		Total:	$

EXPENSE TRACKER: WEEK 5

Date	Description	Is It Needed? (Y/N)	Amount
			$
			$
			$
			$
			$
			$
			$
			$
			$
			$
			$
			$
			$
			$
			$
			$
			$
			$
			$
			$
			$
			$
			$
			$
			$
		Total:	$

MONTHLY REVIEW

	1. Needed	2. Not Needed	Total Spending (1+2)
Week 1			
Week 2			
Week 3			
Week 4			
Week 5			
Total			

Money Available This Month

Total Spending This Month

Money Saved This Month!

[ ] − [ ] = [ ]

HOW WELL DID YOU DO THIS MONTH? ☆ ☆ ☆ ☆ ☆

HOW TO SAVE EVEN MORE NEXT MONTH?

_____

_____

_____

_____

MONTH

MONTHLY INCOME

Date	Description	Amount
		$
		$
		$
		$
		$
	Total:	$

MONTHLY FIXED EXPENSES

Date	Description	Amount
		$
		$
		$
		$
		$
		$
		$
		$
		$
		$
		$
		$
		$
		$
	Total:	$

MY SAVINGS TARGET FOR THIS MONTH IS

$

MONEY AVAILABLE

Income		Fixed Expenses		Savings Goal		Money Available
	−		−		=	

ESTIMATED SPENDING MONEY

	Week 1	Week 2	Week 3	Week 4	Week 5
Date					
Estimated Spending Money					
Expenses					

NOTES

_____

_____

_____

_____

_____

EXPENSE TRACKER: WEEK 1

Date	Description	Is It Needed? (Y/N)	Amount
			$
			$
			$
			$
			$
			$
			$
			$
			$
			$
			$
			$
			$
			$
			$
			$
			$
			$
			$
			$
			$
			$
			$
			$
			$
			$
		Total:	$

EXPENSE TRACKER: WEEK 2

Date	Description	Is It Needed? (Y/N)	Amount
			$
			$
			$
			$
			$
			$
			$
			$
			$
			$
			$
			$
			$
			$
			$
			$
			$
			$
			$
			$
			$
			$
			$
			$
			$
			$
		Total:	$

EXPENSE TRACKER: WEEK 3

Date	Description	Is It Needed? (Y/N)	Amount
			$
			$
			$
			$
			$
			$
			$
			$
			$
			$
			$
			$
			$
			$
			$
			$
			$
			$
			$
			$
			$
			$
			$
			$
			$
			$
		Total:	$

EXPENSE TRACKER: WEEK 4

Date	Description	Is It Needed? (Y/N)	Amount
			$
			$
			$
			$
			$
			$
			$
			$
			$
			$
			$
			$
			$
			$
			$
			$
			$
			$
			$
			$
			$
			$
			$
			$
			$
			$
			$
		Total:	$

EXPENSE TRACKER: WEEK 5

Date	Description	Is It Needed? (Y/N)	Amount
			$
			$
			$
			$
			$
			$
			$
			$
			$
			$
			$
			$
			$
			$
			$
			$
			$
			$
			$
			$
			$
			$
			$
			$
			$
			$
		Total:	$

MONTHLY REVIEW

	1. Needed	2. Not Needed	Total Spending (1+2)
Week 1			
Week 2			
Week 3			
Week 4			
Week 5			
Total			

Money Available This Month

Total Spending This Month

Money Saved This Month!

[ ] − [ ] = [ ]

HOW WELL DID YOU DO THIS MONTH? ☆ ☆ ☆ ☆ ☆

HOW TO SAVE EVEN MORE NEXT MONTH?

_____

_____

_____

_____

MONTH

MONTHLY INCOME

Date	Description	Amount
		$
		$
		$
		$
		$
Total:		$

MONTHLY FIXED EXPENSES

Date	Description	Amount
		$
		$
		$
		$
		$
		$
		$
		$
		$
		$
		$
		$
		$
		$
		$
Total:		$

MY SAVINGS TARGET FOR THIS MONTH IS

	$

MONEY AVAILABLE

Income		Fixed Expenses		Savings Goal		Money Available
☐	−	☐	−	☐	=	☐

ESTIMATED SPENDING MONEY

	Week 1	Week 2	Week 3	Week 4	Week 5
Date					
Estimated Spending Money					
Expenses					

NOTES

_____

_____

_____

_____

_____

EXPENSE TRACKER: WEEK 1

Date	Description	Is It Needed? (Y/N)	Amount
			$
			$
			$
			$
			$
			$
			$
			$
			$
			$
			$
			$
			$
			$
			$
			$
			$
			$
			$
			$
			$
			$
			$
			$
			$
		Total:	$

EXPENSE TRACKER: WEEK 2

Date	Description	Is It Needed? (Y/N)	Amount
			$
			$
			$
			$
			$
			$
			$
			$
			$
			$
			$
			$
			$
			$
			$
			$
			$
			$
			$
			$
			$
			$
			$
			$
			$
			$
		Total:	$

EXPENSE TRACKER: WEEK 3

Date	Description	Is It Needed? (Y/N)	Amount
			$
			$
			$
			$
			$
			$
			$
			$
			$
			$
			$
			$
			$
			$
			$
			$
			$
			$
			$
			$
			$
			$
			$
			$
			$
			$
		Total:	$

EXPENSE TRACKER: WEEK 4

Date	Description	Is It Needed? (Y/N)	Amount
			$
			$
			$
			$
			$
			$
			$
			$
			$
			$
			$
			$
			$
			$
			$
			$
			$
			$
			$
			$
			$
			$
			$
			$
			$
		Total:	$

EXPENSE TRACKER: WEEK 5

Date	Description	Is It Needed? (Y/N)	Amount
			$
			$
			$
			$
			$
			$
			$
			$
			$
			$
			$
			$
			$
			$
			$
			$
			$
			$
			$
			$
			$
			$
			$
			$
			$
			$
			$
		Total:	$

MONTHLY REVIEW

	1. Needed	2. Not Needed	Total Spending (1+2)
Week 1			
Week 2			
Week 3			
Week 4			
Week 5			
Total			

Money Available This Month

Total Spending This Month

Money Saved This Month!

[ ] − [ ] = [ ]

HOW WELL DID YOU DO THIS MONTH? ☆ ☆ ☆ ☆ ☆

HOW TO SAVE EVEN MORE NEXT MONTH?

_____

_____

_____

_____

MONTH

SAVINGS ACCOUNT
(Beginning of Month)

$

MONTHLY INCOME

Date	Description	Amount
		$
		$
		$
		$
		$
	Total:	$

MONTHLY FIXED EXPENSES

Date	Description	Amount
		$
		$
		$
		$
		$
		$
		$
		$
		$
		$
		$
		$
		$
		$
		$
	Total:	$

MY SAVINGS TARGET FOR THIS MONTH IS

$

MONEY AVAILABLE

Income		Fixed Expenses		Savings Goal		Money Available
	−		−		=	

ESTIMATED SPENDING MONEY

	Week 1	Week 2	Week 3	Week 4	Week 5
Date					
Estimated Spending Money					
Expenses					

NOTES

_____

_____

_____

_____

_____

EXPENSE TRACKER: WEEK 1

Date	Description	Is It Needed? (Y/N)	Amount
			$
			$
			$
			$
			$
			$
			$
			$
			$
			$
			$
			$
			$
			$
			$
			$
			$
			$
			$
			$
			$
			$
			$
			$
			$
		Total:	$

EXPENSE TRACKER: WEEK 2

Date	Description	Is It Needed? (Y/N)	Amount
			$
			$
			$
			$
			$
			$
			$
			$
			$
			$
			$
			$
			$
			$
			$
			$
			$
			$
			$
			$
			$
			$
			$
			$
			$
		Total:	$

EXPENSE TRACKER: WEEK 3

Date	Description	Is It Needed? (Y/N)	Amount
			$
			$
			$
			$
			$
			$
			$
			$
			$
			$
			$
			$
			$
			$
			$
			$
			$
			$
			$
			$
			$
			$
			$
			$
			$
			$
		Total:	$

EXPENSE TRACKER: WEEK 4

Date	Description	Is It Needed? (Y/N)	Amount
			$
			$
			$
			$
			$
			$
			$
			$
			$
			$
			$
			$
			$
			$
			$
			$
			$
			$
			$
			$
			$
			$
			$
			$
			$
			$
		Total:	$

EXPENSE TRACKER: WEEK 5

Date	Description	Is It Needed? (Y/N)	Amount
			$
			$
			$
			$
			$
			$
			$
			$
			$
			$
			$
			$
			$
			$
			$
			$
			$
			$
			$
			$
			$
			$
			$
			$
			$
			$
		Total:	$

MONTHLY REVIEW

	1. Needed	2. Not Needed	Total Spending (1+2)
Week 1			
Week 2			
Week 3			
Week 4			
Week 5			
Total			

Money Available This Month

Total Spending This Month

Money Saved This Month!

☐ − ☐ = ☐

HOW WELL DID YOU DO THIS MONTH? ☆ ☆ ☆ ☆ ☆

HOW TO SAVE EVEN MORE NEXT MONTH?

_____

_____

_____

_____

MONTH

MONTHLY INCOME

Date	Description	Amount
		$
		$
		$
		$
		$
	Total:	$

MONTHLY FIXED EXPENSES

Date	Description	Amount
		$
		$
		$
		$
		$
		$
		$
		$
		$
		$
		$
		$
		$
		$
	Total:	$

MY SAVINGS TARGET FOR THIS MONTH IS

$

MONEY AVAILABLE

Income		Fixed Expenses		Savings Goal		Money Available
	−		−		=	

ESTIMATED SPENDING MONEY

	Week 1	Week 2	Week 3	Week 4	Week 5
Date					
Estimated Spending Money					
Expenses					

NOTES

_____

_____

_____

_____

_____

EXPENSE TRACKER: WEEK 1

Date	Description	Is It Needed? (Y/N)	Amount
			$
			$
			$
			$
			$
			$
			$
			$
			$
			$
			$
			$
			$
			$
			$
			$
			$
			$
			$
			$
			$
			$
			$
			$
			$
			$
			$
		Total:	$

EXPENSE TRACKER: WEEK 2

Date	Description	Is It Needed? (Y/N)	Amount
			$
			$
			$
			$
			$
			$
			$
			$
			$
			$
			$
			$
			$
			$
			$
			$
			$
			$
			$
			$
			$
			$
			$
			$
			$
			$
		Total:	$

EXPENSE TRACKER: WEEK 3

Date	Description	Is It Needed? (Y/N)	Amount
			$
			$
			$
			$
			$
			$
			$
			$
			$
			$
			$
			$
			$
			$
			$
			$
			$
			$
			$
			$
			$
			$
			$
			$
			$
			$
		Total:	$

EXPENSE TRACKER: WEEK 4

Date	Description	Is It Needed? (Y/N)	Amount
			$
			$
			$
			$
			$
			$
			$
			$
			$
			$
			$
			$
			$
			$
			$
			$
			$
			$
			$
			$
			$
			$
			$
			$
			$
			$
			$
		Total:	$

EXPENSE TRACKER: WEEK 5

Date	Description	Is It Needed? (Y/N)	Amount
			$
			$
			$
			$
			$
			$
			$
			$
			$
			$
			$
			$
			$
			$
			$
			$
			$
			$
			$
			$
			$
			$
			$
			$
			$
		Total:	$

MONTHLY REVIEW

	1. Needed	2. Not Needed	Total Spending (1+2)
Week 1			
Week 2			
Week 3			
Week 4			
Week 5			
Total			

Money Available This Month − **Total Spending This Month** = **Money Saved This Month!**

HOW WELL DID YOU DO THIS MONTH? ☆ ☆ ☆ ☆ ☆

HOW TO SAVE EVEN MORE NEXT MONTH?

_____

_____

_____

_____

MONTH

SAVINGS ACCOUNT
(Beginning of Month)
$

MONTHLY INCOME

Date	Description	Amount
		$
		$
		$
		$
		$
	Total:	$

MONTHLY FIXED EXPENSES

Date	Description	Amount
		$
		$
		$
		$
		$
		$
		$
		$
		$
		$
		$
		$
		$
		$
		$
	Total:	$

MY SAVINGS TARGET FOR THIS MONTH IS

$

MONEY AVAILABLE

Income		Fixed Expenses		Savings Goal		Money Available
	–		–		=	

ESTIMATED SPENDING MONEY

	Week 1	Week 2	Week 3	Week 4	Week 5
Date					
Estimated Spending Money					
Expenses					

NOTES

_____

_____

_____

_____

_____

EXPENSE TRACKER: WEEK 1

Date	Description	Is It Needed? (Y/N)	Amount
			$
			$
			$
			$
			$
			$
			$
			$
			$
			$
			$
			$
			$
			$
			$
			$
			$
			$
			$
			$
			$
			$
			$
			$
			$
		Total:	$

EXPENSE TRACKER: WEEK 2

Date	Description	Is It Needed? (Y/N)	Amount
			$
			$
			$
			$
			$
			$
			$
			$
			$
			$
			$
			$
			$
			$
			$
			$
			$
			$
			$
			$
			$
			$
			$
			$
			$
		Total:	$

EXPENSE TRACKER: WEEK 3

Date	Description	Is It Needed? (Y/N)	Amount
			$
			$
			$
			$
			$
			$
			$
			$
			$
			$
			$
			$
			$
			$
			$
			$
			$
			$
			$
			$
			$
			$
			$
			$
			$
			$
		Total:	$

EXPENSE TRACKER: WEEK 4

Date	Description	Is It Needed? (Y/N)	Amount
			$
			$
			$
			$
			$
			$
			$
			$
			$
			$
			$
			$
			$
			$
			$
			$
			$
			$
			$
			$
			$
			$
			$
			$
			$
			$
		Total:	$

EXPENSE TRACKER: WEEK 5

Date	Description	Is It Needed? (Y/N)	Amount
			$
			$
			$
			$
			$
			$
			$
			$
			$
			$
			$
			$
			$
			$
			$
			$
			$
			$
			$
			$
			$
			$
			$
			$
			$
			$
			$
		Total:	$

MONTHLY REVIEW

	1. Needed	2. Not Needed	Total Spending (1+2)
Week 1			
Week 2			
Week 3			
Week 4			
Week 5			
Total			

Money Available This Month − **Total Spending This Month** = **Money Saved This Month!**

HOW WELL DID YOU DO THIS MONTH? ☆ ☆ ☆ ☆ ☆

HOW TO SAVE EVEN MORE NEXT MONTH?

_____

_____

_____

_____

Made in United States
Troutdale, OR
04/18/2024

19267896R00061